McDougal Littell

LITERATURE IN PERFORMANCE

BRITISH LITERATURE

VIDEO RESOURCE BOOK

A VIDEO COMPANION TO
The Language of Literature

A HOUGHTON MIFFLIN COMPANY

Evanston, Illinois Boston Dallas

ISBN 0-395-97249-3

Printed in the United States of America.

3 4 5 6 7 8 9 — BEI — 03 02 01 00

Contents

Introduction

WELCOME TO LITERATURE IN PERFORMANCE

Literature in Performance is a companion video series for *The Language of Literature*. The series features great film performances of both classic and contemporary works presented in the textbooks.

There is nothing like a performance to spark appreciation for words on a page, awareness of different interpretations, and lively class discussion. This is the purpose of ***Literature in Performance***—to help bring literature to life through film adaptations and to create an opportunity for students to compare and contrast performances with literary texts.

Literature in Performance is designed to take students beyond texts and into the media of film and video. It can aid in the development of students' listening and viewing skills, improve their media literacy, and increase their familiarity with different literary genres.

As you and your students explore ***Literature in Performance,*** may you find the journey exciting and inspiring!

COMPONENTS OF THE PROGRAM

The ***Literature in Performance*** video series includes the following components:

Videocassette The videocassette for each grade contains at least six performances preceded by narrative introductions.

Teacher's Resource Book This is your guide to using the program. The resources in this book include the following materials:

- background information that provides interesting facts about the performances
- previewing questions and activities that create a focus for students' viewing
- discussion questions for use after students view the performances
- writing options and reproducible extension activities
- annotated lists of related films, videos, and CD-ROMs
- a glossary of film terms, a list of resources for teaching with film, and three general viewing activities

USING *LITERATURE IN PERFORMANCE* IN THE CLASSROOM

Literature in Performance is designed to enhance your teaching of literature. If you are using *The Language of Literature,* you will find that the videos on each cassette are related to specific selections in the student textbook. For example, the video *The Rocking Horse Winner* presents an adaptation of D. H. Lawrence's short story in Unit 6, Part 1, of the British Literature *Language of Literature* textbook. The lessons in this book assume that students will have read the selections before viewing the videos.

When you wish to use a video, the following suggestions may help you:

- **Lesson at a Glance** Found at the beginning of each lesson, this list of objectives and activities is intended to help you plan your use of the lesson.
- **Before Viewing** You may preview a performance by watching it or by reading the Building Background material in this book. You may wish to use the Tapping Prior Knowledge activity, which includes a graphic organizer and prompts students to discuss ideas related to the selection and the performance. Focus for Viewing can help to focus students' approach to the performance they are about to see, and Before Viewing introduces points of comparison between the text and the performance, as well as a literary concept that can be applied to the performance.
- **Viewing** Encourage students to be active viewers and to jot down questions and impressions as they watch a performance. Consider allowing them to view the performance a second time to study a particular scene or image. A Viewer's Guide copymaster, which includes a graphic organizer, is provided for students to use while initially viewing the performance or while viewing it a second time.
- **After Viewing** Because each video is approximately 10 to 20 minutes long, there is ample time for discussion after viewing. Use the questions on the After Viewing page to initiate discussion. (Answers are included on the page.) The After Viewing page also includes a Writing Option tied to the lesson.
- **Extension Activities** You may wish to extend the lesson with the copymasters that follow the After Viewing page. These allow students to engage in activities such as planning a film adaptation, evaluating the composition of film frames, and analyzing film reviews. Answers to the questions are located in the back of this book.
- **Additional Resources** If your students want to study another performance, refer them to the films, videos, and CD-ROMs in the Additional Resources section.

At the back of this book, you will find a Film Glossary to help you with unfamiliar filmmaking terms. Resources for Teaching with Film suggests a number of resources that can help you further explore the use of film in your classroom. When presenting additional performances or films in class, you may wish to provide students with one or more of the three Viewing Activity copymasters.

from Beowulf

The Battle with Grendel

A STORYTELLING PERFORMANCE BY SYD LIEBERMAN

"Beowulf *has all the ingredients of a wonderful tale—blood and gore, drama, good versus evil.*"

—STORYTELLER SYD LIEBERMAN

LESSON AT A GLANCE

Overview

In this videotaped performance, storyteller Syd Lieberman retells in his own unique style the story of Beowulf's battle with Grendel.

Running Time: 9:30

Connecting to *The Language of Literature*

Show this video after students read *Beowulf* in Unit 1, Part 1.

Objectives

- To compare the text of *Beowulf* with a performed version
- To understand how characterization is developed in a storytelling performance
- To analyze a storyteller's use of words, voice, and body language
- To select, prepare, and present a story to an audience

Lesson Activities

- Writing Option: Write a Review (page 6)
- Viewer's Guide: The Art of Storytelling (page 7)
- Extension Activity: Weave a Tale (page 8)

Before Viewing

Storyteller Syd Lieberman

BUILDING BACKGROUND

In this video performance, storyteller Syd Lieberman tells the legendary tale of Beowulf's battle with the monster Grendel. "It's the first story in our language," says Lieberman, explaining his interest in the tale, "and, of all things, it's a monster story. There's something about scary tales that people love. *Beowulf* has all the ingredients of a wonderful tale—blood and gore, drama, good versus evil." Lieberman enjoys bringing this ancient story alive for audiences. "I try to have the audience imagine they are around a camp fire or in a mead hall."

Lieberman is an English teacher at Evanston Township High School in Evanston, Illinois. He is also a professional storyteller who has performed at festivals around the world. He is the author of *Streets and Alleys: Stories with a Chicago Accent* and has recorded audiotapes of his work, including *The Tell-Tale Heart and Other Terrifying Tales.*

TAPPING PRIOR KNOWLEDGE

Starting with the Student Ask students to think of someone they know who can tell a good story. What does this person do to create entertaining stories? Have students use a word web like the one below to record their thoughts.

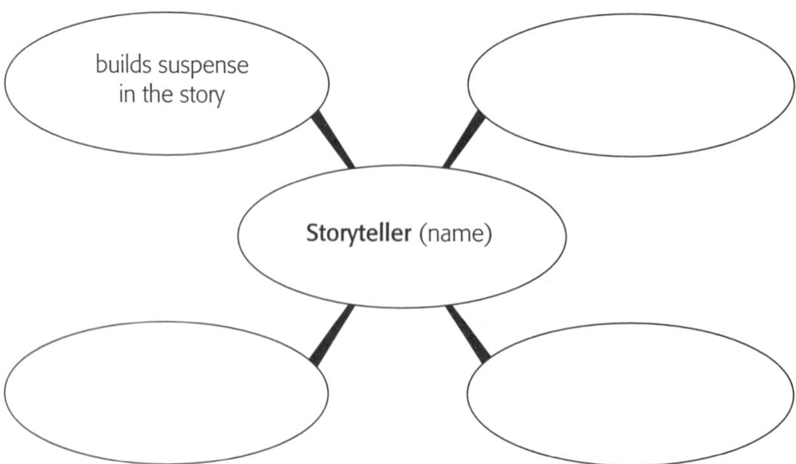

FOCUS FOR VIEWING

The Art of Storytelling Discuss the following question with students: What do good storytellers think about as they plan and prepare for a performance? Lead students to consider the following aspects of a storytelling performance:

- the use of specific **words**, phrases, and lines that convey key images
- the use of **voice** to create a dramatic effect
- the use of **body language** to bring the characters and actions alive

Encourage students to think about the following question as they view Syd Lieberman's performance of the *Beowulf* story: What techniques does the storyteller use to make his story effective?

(You may wish to have students use the Viewer's Guide on page 7 to record their observations.)

COMPARING TEXT AND PERFORMANCE

Ask students to look for the similarities and differences between the *Beowulf* story that they read and the one they are about to view, especially noting the following comparisons:

- differences in plot
- differences in how the characters are portrayed

LITERARY ANALYSIS IN MEDIA

Characterization A writer develops a character by using such techniques as describing the character's appearance, thoughts, and actions. A storyteller also uses specific techniques to develop a character. Encourage students to consider the following questions as they view the storyteller's performance: What body language and sounds does the storyteller use to portray the characters in the story? How does the storyteller switch characters?

Additional Resources: Storytelling

The Tell-Tale Heart and Other Terrifying Tales
Syd Lieberman tells classic tales including *Beowulf*, "The Tell-Tale Heart," "The Occurrence at Owl Creek Bridge." *(Audiocassette, 52 minutes, available through Syd Lieberman, 2522 Ashland Avenue, Evanston, Illinois, 60201)*

The 20th Anniversary National Storytelling Festival: A Commemorative Documentary
This documentary examines the craft of storytelling and includes interviews and performances by some of America's best storytellers. *(Videocassette, 20 minutes, 1995; distributor: Hometown Entertainment (800) 786-7983)*

After Viewing

Use these prompts to initiate discussion after viewing:

WHAT DO YOU THINK?

1. What moments from Syd Lieberman's story stand out in your mind? (Answers will vary.)

FOCUS FOR VIEWING

2. **The Art of Storytelling** What techniques did the storyteller use to make his performance effective? Think about his word choice, delivery, body language, and gestures. (Vivid word choice to describe the action; lowering and raising his voice to heighten the drama; use of his hands and arms to show important moments.)

COMPARING TEXT AND PERFORMANCE

3. **Plot** What plot details were added to or deleted from the performance? Do you think these changes improved the story? (Added: Physical descriptions of Beowulf and Grendel and the gifts from the king to Beowulf after the battle. Deleted: Descriptive material such as family history and scenes unrelated to the battle.)
4. **Character** How were the storyteller's descriptions of Beowulf and Grendel different from the text's descriptions? (The storyteller added physical descriptions: Beowulf is a huge man with large shoulders and big hands. Grendel is "two or three times six feet tall" with one red eye and one yellow eye.)

LITERARY ANALYSIS IN MEDIA

5. **Characterization** Describe the body language and sounds that the storyteller used to portray each character. (For Beowulf, the storyteller called attention to his arms and hands and used a proud stance and flashing eyes. For Grendel, he adopted a hungry expression and because Grendel is a giant, he looked down.)

LESSON ACTIVITIES

- **Writing Option: Write a Review** Ask students to imagine they are critics and have them write a brief review of the storyteller's performance. Have them support their opinions with examples.
- **Viewer's Guide: The Art of Storytelling** Use the copymaster on page 7 to have students analyze storytelling techniques in the performance.
- **Extension Activity: Weave a Tale** Use the copymaster on page 8 to help students develop storytelling performances of their own.

Name: ______________________ Date: ____________

VIEWER'S GUIDE

THE ART OF STORYTELLING

An instructor once told Syd Lieberman, "If you're not going to do something special while you tell a story, you should hand out copies of your story and ask the audience to read it instead!" Professional storytellers like Lieberman carefully plan and practice their performances. View *The Battle with Grendel*, watching closely for the storyteller's word choices, his delivery, and his body language. Use the chart below to record your observations.

Words Jot down the words, phrases, and sentences from the performance that helped create vivid images.	
Delivery Describe the tone of voice that the storyteller used for each character. Describe how the pace and volume of his speech changed during the story.	
Body Language Describe the gestures, postures, and facial expressions that helped you to visualize the characters and scenes.	

Name: ______________________________ Date: ______________

EXTENSION ACTIVITY

WEAVE A TALE

Now it's your turn to be a storyteller.

Step 1 Choose a story. Consider personal experiences, family lore, ghosts stories, or a tale from your literature textbook.

Step 2 Plan your delivery. Use the chart below to help you organize your ideas. Record your ideas in a rough script or on index cards.

Step 3 Practice your story in front of a mirror or have a friend videotape it. Pay attention to your body language and facial expressions.

Step 4 Perform your story for the class.

"I cut out much of the history from the written version because it doesn't matter to a modern audience. I left only the 'straight line' of the battle scene."

—Lieberman on adapting the story

Planning Guide	
What are the parts or scenes of the story?	
What details will you include?	
What words and phrases do you want to be sure to use?	
How will you vary the tone, volume, and pace of your voice in telling the story?	
What gestures and facial expressions do you want to use to make the characters and scenes come alive?	

from The Canterbury Tales

The Pardoner's Tale

A FILM ADAPTATION NARRATED BY SIR JOHN GIELGUD

"Don't think I can't tell moral tales. I can! Here's one I often preach"

—FROM "THE PARDONER'S PROLOGUE" BY GEOFFREY CHAUCER

LESSON AT A GLANCE

Overview

Geoffrey Chaucer's "The Pardoner's Tale" is dramatized in a film adaptation.

Running Time: 15:00

Connecting to *The Language of Literature*

Show this video after students read "The Pardoner's Tale" and the Author Study on Chaucer in Unit 1, Part 2.

Objectives

- To compare Chaucer's "The Pardoner's Tale" with the film adaptation
- To understand how personification is developed in a film
- To analyze how a piece of literature is adapted to film
- To plan the film adaptation of a scene from literature

Lesson Activities

- Writing Option: Rewrite a Scene (page 12)
- Viewer's Guide: Adapting a Story to Film (page 13)
- Extension Activity: From Page to Screen (page 14)

Before Viewing

Three rioters plot to kill Death in "The Pardoner's Tale."

BUILDING BACKGROUND

This film is a modern adaptation of Geoffrey Chaucer's "The Pardoner's Tale," one of the liveliest stories in *The Canterbury Tales*. The film comes from *Six Centuries of Verse,* a 16-part British television series about the history of English poetry. In the original TV series, this performance of "The Pardoner's Tale" followed a biography of Chaucer and a performance of the prologue to the tale spoken in Middle English. The series was produced in 1984 by British Thames Television. The creator of the series, Anthony Thwaite, said he would like students to understand "how entertaining and skillful Chaucer is." The script for "The Pardoner's Tale" is based on Nevill Coghill's modern verse translation. Shakespearean actor Sir John Gielgud reads the part of the Pardoner in Chaucer's brisk rhyming couplets. An Academy Award winner, Gielgud appears as host for the series as well.

TAPPING PRIOR KNOWLEDGE

Thinking About the Text Ask students to imagine that they are making a film of "The Pardoner's Tale." Based on their reading of the poem, what would the Pardoner look like? What physical characteristics should the actor have and how would he be dressed? Also, what would the setting be like? What props and scenery should be included in the staging of the story? Have students use a chart like the one below to record their descriptions.

Actor's appearance
Costume
Setting
Props
Scenery

This adaptation is excerpted from *A Survey of English Poetry: Chaucer. (Videocassette, 28 minutes, 1984; distributor: Films for the Humanities, (800) 257-5126)*

FOCUS FOR VIEWING

Adapting a Story to Film Explain to students that when a piece of literature is made into a film, the filmmaker faces several initial questions. Among the most important of these questions are the following:

- To what extent should changes be made in a story's **language** or **plot**?
- Which actors should be in the **cast** and how should they be **costumed**?
- How should each scene be **staged**?

As the students view "The Pardoner's Tale," have them note how each of the above questions was answered. (You may wish to have students use the Viewer's Guide on page 13 to note their observations.)

COMPARING TEXT AND PERFORMANCE

Encourage students to look for the similarities and differences between "The Pardoner's Tale" that they read and the one they are viewing, especially noting the following comparisons:

- the appearance and role of the Pardoner
- the language that is used in both the poem and the film

LITERARY ANALYSIS IN MEDIA

Personification Personification is a figure of speech in which human qualities are attributed to an object, animal, or idea. Chaucer uses personification in "The Pardoner's Tale" when he makes Death a character in the poem.

There came a privy thief, they call him Death,
Who kills us all round here, and in a breath
He speared him through the heart, he never stirred.
And then Death went his way without a word.

Encourage students to think about how Death is personified in the film adaptation of Chaucer's poem.

Additional Resources: The Theme of Betrayal

Becket

This film chronicles the relationship between Thomas à Becket, the archbishop of Canterbury, and King Henry II. A rift with the greedy king leads to the archbishop's martyrdom. The film explains the origin of the pilgrimage in Chaucer's *The Canterbury Tales* and features Richard Burton and Peter O'Toole. *(Videocassette, 148 minutes, 1964; distributor: Critics' Choice Video, (800) 367-7765)*

The Treasure of the Sierra Madre

Adapted from the novel by B. Traven and starring Walter Huston and Humphrey Bogart, this film is a classic retelling of "The Pardoner's Tale." Set in Mexico, three opportunists find gold, betrayal, and greed in the mountains of the Sierra Madre. *(Videocassette, 126 minutes, 1948; distributor: Critics' Choice Video, (800) 367-7765)*

After Viewing

Use these prompts to initiate discussion:

WHAT DO YOU THINK?

1. Which scene in the film did you find most interesting? (Possible answers: the tavern scene, the murder scene.)

FOCUS FOR VIEWING

2. **Adapting a Story to Film** What did you think of the actors, costumes, and settings chosen for this film? (Answers will vary.)

COMPARING TEXT AND PERFORMANCE

3. **The Pardoner** How did the Pardoner in the film differ from the Pardoner in Chaucer's poem? (The Pardoner in the film was the narrator. He was not a character. He had modern clothes and read from a book.)
4. **Language** Compare the words in the film with those in the poem. (The language was unchanged. Some students might note that one page of the Pardoner's lines at the end of the story had been left out of the film.)

LITERARY ANALYSIS IN MEDIA

5. **Personification** Describe how Death was personified in the film. (Death was personified as an old man dressed in a black hooded robe.)

LESSON ACTIVITIES

- **Writing Option: Rewrite a Scene** Ask Students to choose one scene in "The Pardoner's Tale"—such as the tavern scene or the murder scene—and rewrite it in modern English.
- **Viewer's Guide: Adapting a Story to Film** Students may use the copymaster on page 13 to note the choices that the filmmaker made in the adaptation of "The Pardoner's Tale."
- **Extension Activity: From Page to Screen** Students may use the copymaster on page 14 to plan a film adaptation of a scene from literature.

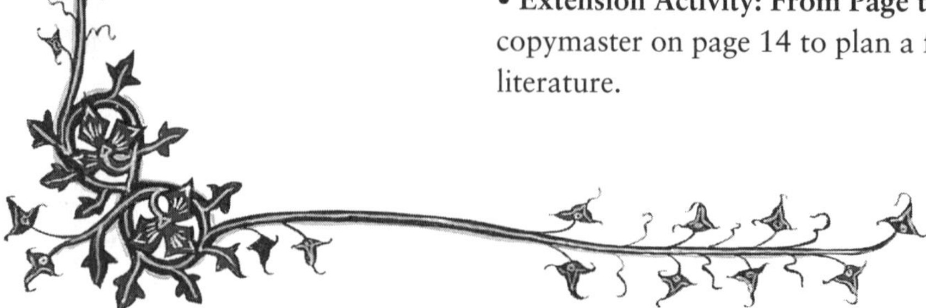

Name: ______________________ Date: __________

VIEWER'S GUIDE

ADAPTING A STORY TO FILM

When adapting a piece of literature to film, a filmmaker must consider several important elements, including the script, cast, costumes, and setting. In planning these elements, the filmmaker seeks to use the power of images and sound to interpret the story in an interesting way.

View the "The Pardoner's Tale" and note how the filmmaker handled each of these elements. Use the chart below to record your observations.

Observations	
• Why do you think the filmmaker chose not to change Chaucer's wording when creating the **script**?	
• Describe the **cast.** To what extent did they help you visualize Chaucer's poem?	
• Describe the **costumes.** Why do you think this type of costume was chosen?	
• Describe the **settings.** What were your impressions of the settings chosen?	

Name: ______________________________ Date: ______________

EXTENSION ACTIVITY

FROM PAGE TO SCREEN

Many people are involved in the adaptation of a story to a film. Several of the roles that contribute to the creation are described in the chart below.

Role	Job Description
Costumes	Designs and purchases the costumes for each character in the film
Set	Designs and builds the set for each scene
Casting	Chooses and hires the cast
Music	Writes music for the film or chooses existing music

In teams of four, chose a scene from literature that you would like to adapt for film. Have each group member assume a role from the list and plan how one aspect of the film should be handled. For example, the person in charge of the set will brainstorm with the group about what the setting of the scene should look like. Use the chart below to record your group's plans.

Story title:______________________________

Describe the choices you made	Explain the effect you want to create
Costumes	
Set	
Casting	
Music	

from Macbeth

A FILM ADAPTATION BY ORSON WELLES AND A VIDEOTAPED STAGE PRODUCTION BY THE ROYAL SHAKESPEARE COMPANY

Orson Welles as Macbeth

Ian McKellen as Macbeth

LESSON AT A GLANCE

Overview

The prophecy scene of *Macbeth* is performed in an Orson Welles film adaptation and in a Royal Shakespeare Company stage production videotaped for television.

Running Times: 9:30 and 7:30

Connecting to *The Language of Literature*

Show these performances after students read *Macbeth* and the Author Study on Shakespeare in Unit 2, Part 2.

Objectives

- To compare the text of Shakespeare's *Macbeth,* Act 1, Scene 3, with the Welles and Royal Shakespeare scenes.
- To understand how asides are handled in film and on stage
- To analyze the role of the camera in film productions

Lesson Activities

- Writing Option: Actor's Notes (page 18)
- Viewer's Guide: The Camera (page 19)
- Extension Activity 1: Compare and Contrast Performances (page 20)
- Extension Activity 2: Evaluate Movie Reviews (page 21)
- Extension Activity 3: The Art of Acting (page 22)

Before Viewing

The three witches in Royal Shakespeare Company's *Macbeth*

BUILDING BACKGROUND

Scenes from a film adaptation and a stage production of Shakespeare's *Macbeth*, showing excerpts from Act I, are presented for comparison.

The first performance—the prophecy scene from a 1948 film adaptation of *Macbeth*—was produced by the pioneering U.S. director Orson Welles. Welles not only directed and produced the film, he also wrote the film script and played the role of Macbeth. Although the play is set in ancient Scotland, the film was shot on a sound stage in about three weeks on a very small budget. Welles made many changes to Shakespeare's play, such as cutting and rearranging scenes and altering lines. He characterized this shortened, simplified version as "a violently sketched charcoal drawing of a great play."

The second performance features the *Macbeth* prophecy scene staged by the Royal Shakespeare Company and directed by Britain's Trevor Nunn. Nunn's *Macbeth* was first broadcast on television in 1979 and featured Ian McKellen as Macbeth. The play was a bare-bones production with minimal props and virtually no scenery. Nunn used lighting to illuminate the actors within a circular performance space. The minimal setting placed greater emphasis on the acting to carry the story. Nunn explained, "There was only one location, and that location was being transformed into different places by people who were enacting the story."

TAPPING PRIOR KNOWLEDGE

Thinking About the Text Ask students to think about how Shakespeare portrayed the witches and Macbeth's reaction to their prophecies. How do students think Macbeth looks when he hears this news? Stunned? Elated? Confused? Have students use a graphic organizer like the one below to describe Macbeth's reactions.

Macbeth hears the prophecy that he will be king.	→	**Macbeth's reactions**
		______________________
		______________________
		______________________
		______________________
		______________________
		______________________
		______________________

This film adaptation is excerpted from *Macbeth. (Videocassette, 112 minutes, 1948; distributor: Critics' Choice Video, (800) 367-7765)*

This stage production is excerpted from *Macbeth. (Videocassette, 150 minutes, 1979; distributor: Films for the Humanities, (800) 257-5126)*

FOCUS FOR VIEWING

The Camera Discuss with students the camera shots used in the film excerpts, including the following types:

- An **establishing shot** is one that sets the location of a story or scene. It is often a long, wide-angle view of an area.
- A **close-up** is a shot taken at close range, giving a magnified view of a character or an object in a scene. Close-ups that focus on the face of a character are used to reveal the character's feelings. Close-ups of objects are used to emphasize their significance in the plot or to establish them as symbols.
- A **low-angle shot** is one that looks up at a character or a subject from a camera position below the eye level of the subject. Low-angle shots can give a subject or character an illusion of dominance.

As students view both prophecy scenes, have them note the kinds of camera shots used and the effects these shots achieved. (You may wish to have students use the Viewer's Guide on page 19 to note their observations of Welles's film.)

COMPARING TEXT AND PERFORMANCE

Ask students to look for similarities and differences between the *Macbeth* prophecy scene that they read and the two performances they will view, especially noting the following points of comparison:

- the way the witches are portrayed
- the setting
- the actors' interpretation of Macbeth
- the language

LITERARY ANALYSIS IN MEDIA

Aside In drama, an aside is a remark spoken in an undertone by a character, either to the audience or to another character. A traditional dramatic convention, the aside is heard by the audience but supposedly not by other characters on stage. Asides can be used to express characters' feelings, opinions, and reactions, and so function as a method of characterization. In *Macbeth,* Shakespeare includes several asides in the prophecy scene to reveal Macbeth's reactions to the witches' predictions. Encourage students to speculate on how the asides will be handled in the two films. What additional techniques do filmmakers have to create asides?

Additional Resources: Macbeth

Macbeth

This multimedia CD-ROM includes listings of characters, annotations, expert commentary, a full audio recording, excerpts from film versions, and a *Macbeth* karaoke, which allows students to play various roles alongside professional actors. *(CD-ROM, 1994; distributor: Educorp, (800) 843-9497)*

Throne of Blood

Akira Kurosawa's film recasts *Macbeth* as a samurai epic to reflect the politics and intrigues of medieval Japan. Includes English subtitles. *(Videocassette, 105 minutes, 1957; distributor: Critics' Choice Video, (800) 367-7765)*

After Viewing

Use these prompts to initiate discussion after viewing:

WHAT DO YOU THINK?

1. Which version of the prophecy scene did you think was more effective? Why? (Answers will vary.)

FOCUS FOR VIEWING

2. **The Camera** Describe one kind of camera shot (establishing shot, close-up, or low-angle) that you noticed in the Welles film excerpt. Explain its purpose and effect. (An establishing shot was used in the opening to show the location of the witches on a foggy moor. It set the mood.)

COMPARING TEXT AND PERFORMANCE

3. **Portrayal of the Witches** How were the witches portrayed in Shakespeare's play and in the two film performances? (Shakespeare's text did not describe the witches. In Welles's film, the witches were presented as faceless shapes with shrill voices; in Nunn's production, the witches were shown in scary detail.)
4. **Interpretation of Macbeth** How was Macbeth portrayed differently in the text and the film versions? (In both the text and the Nunn production, Macbeth was portrayed as an ambitious nobleman; in the Welles's film, he was portrayed as a barbarian.)

5. **Language** Compare Shakespeare's wording with that used in the film performances. (The language in Welles's film is simplified and shortened; the Nunn version more closely adheres to the original text.)

LITERARY ANALYSIS IN MEDIA

6. **Aside** Describe how Macbeth's aside was handled in each version. (In Welles's film, Macbeth's thoughts were heard in a voice-over; in the Nunn production, the aside was handled in the traditional stage manner.)

LESSON ACTIVITIES

- **Writing Option: Actor's Notes** Ask students to imagine they are actors preparing to play Macbeth in the prophecy scene. Have them take notes about how they will react to the witches' prophecies.

- **Viewer's Guide: The Camera** Use the copymaster on page 19 to help students analyze the camera shots in Welles's production.
- **Extension Activities 1–3** Use the copymasters on pages 20–22 to help students compare and contrast specific elements of the performances; evaluate critical reviews; and evaluate acting.

Name: ______________________________ Date: ______________

VIEWER'S GUIDE

THE CAMERA

In the 1940s, Orson Welles became known for his innovative filming techniques. View the prophecy scene from *Macbeth* and observe the following camera shots:

- **establishing shot:** a shot that presents a complete view of the setting of a scene—usually a long, wide-angle view
- **close-up:** a shot that presents a tight shot on an object or a character, often focusing from below the shoulder to above the head, especially on the face
- **low-angle shot:** a shot that looks up at a character from below the character's eye level

Use the chart below to describe the camera shot in each scene listed and to explain its effects.

Scene	Describe the camera shot	Explain its effects
Macbeth and Banquo riding up to the witches		
Macbeth and Banquo confronting the witches		
Macbeth speaking with men on horseback		
Macbeth's aside		
Ending view of the witches		

Name: ______________________________ Date: ______________

EXTENSION ACTIVITY 1

COMPARE AND CONTRAST PERFORMANCES

Orson Welles's film *Macbeth* differs significantly from the Royal Shakespeare Company (RSC) production. Note the differences in the chart below, focusing on the elements listed.

Element	Welles's *Macbeth*	RSC's *Macbeth*
Setting		
Portrayal of witches		
Portrayal of Macbeth		
Language		

Name: ______________________ Date: __________

EXTENSION ACTIVITY 2

EVALUATE MOVIE REVIEWS

Critics often have very different opinions about the same performance, as the following reviews show. Do you agree or disagree with the critics? Explain your opinion.

ON ORSON WELLES'S ACTING PERFORMANCE IN *MACBETH*

1. "In the role of Macbeth, Orson Welles proves himself to be a remarkable tragedian, and if the Scottish accent imitated by Americans may be unbearable to English ears, I confess that it did not disturb me."
—Jean Cocteau, "Profile of Orson Welles"

2. "Welles looks more like Atilla the Hun than a courtier, and he goes through the entire picture with a crazed, somnambulistic expression."
—James Naremore, "The Walking Shadow: Welles's Expressionist *Macbeth*"

ON THE ROYAL SHAKESPEARE COMPANY'S *MACBETH*

3. "Yes, that's the way to do Shakespeare, or at least one very good way; limbo lighting, plain speaking, everything in close up, the words gripping as they have rarely gripped before."
—Philip Purser, *The Sunday Telegraph*, January 7, 1979

4. "The absence of background, the unusual, patchy lighting, and the sometimes uncomfortable closeups carry over from the theatre the sense of surrealism and the eerie feeling that there are people nearby . . . the camera moves in close so that the viewer sees the action as if part of it onstage. In themselves no special innovations, such shots and camerawork nevertheless keep the viewer aware that he is within the play, even to the point of being addressed directly in the soliloquies."
—Michael Mullin, "Stage and Screen: The Trevor Nunn *Macbeth*"

Name: ______________________________ Date: ______________

EXTENSION ACTIVITY 3

THE ART OF ACTING

Some critics say that the best acting does not appear to be acting at all. What do you think? What standards can you use to evaluate film acting? The following criteria are often used to judge the quality of acting in film performances:

- **Physical qualities:** Do the actor's movements and facial features attract and hold your attention?
- **Inner spirit:** Does the actor reveal the inner emotions and qualities of the character?
- **Control:** Does the actor create a character without exaggerating the role or acting too restrained?
- **Truth:** Does the actor create a believable character?

Use these criteria to evaluate the acting of Orson Welles and Ian McKellen as Macbeth. Note your comments and rank each performance criterion from 1 to 10, with 10 as highest.

	Orson Welles as Macbeth		Ian McKellen as Macbeth	
	Comments	Rating	Comments	Rating
Physical qualities				
Inner spirit				
Control				
Truth				

Kubla Khan

A READING OF THE POEM WITH PHOTOGRAPHS AND MUSIC

"*In Xanadu did Kubla Khan*
A stately pleasure dome decree:
Where Alph, the sacred river, ran
Through caverns measureless to man
Down to a sunless sea."

—OPENING LINES OF COLERIDGE'S "KUBLA KHAN"

LESSON AT A GLANCE

Overview

Music and photographs are set to a reading of Samuel Taylor Coleridge's famous poem, "Kubla Khan."

Running Time: 6:00

Connecting to *The Language of Literature*

Show this video after students read "Kubla Khan" in Unit 4, Part 1.

Objectives

- To identify and analyze the elements of a montage
- To compare Coleridge's poem with a montage of the poem
- To understand how imagery is developed in a video presentation of a poem

Lesson Activities

- Writing Option: Journal Entry (page 25)
- Viewer's Guide: The Art of Montage (page 26)

Before Viewing

Additional Resources: Samuel Taylor Coleridge

The Rime of the Ancient Mariner
Sir Michael Redgrave narrates this award-winning documentary on Samuel Taylor Coleridge. This documentary includes an interpretation of "The Rime of the Ancient Mariner." *(Videocassette, 60 minutes, 1974; distributor: Kultur International Films Ltd., (800) 458-5887)*

Writing "The Rime of the Ancient Mariner"
This documentary explores aspects of the land and seascapes where Coleridge lived and worked in the English countryside, which inspired his language and imagery. The video features an actor portraying Coleridge, and contemporary comment and readings of parts of "The Rime of the Ancient Mariner." *(Videocassette, 20 minutes, 1992; distributor: Films for the Humanities, (800) 257-5126)*

BUILDING BACKGROUND

This 1997 production sets images and music to a reading of Samuel Taylor Coleridge's evocative poem, "Kubla Khan." The style—a montage of images, music, and narration—is a popular technique used by filmmakers such as Ken Burns in his well-known documentaries on baseball and the American Civil War.

FOCUS FOR VIEWING

The Art of Montage Explain to students that the montage of "Kubla Khan" is an interpretation of Coleridge's famous poem. The editing technique of combining images and music with an oral reading is sometimes referred to as **montage,** from the French word *monter*, meaning "to assemble." A filmmaker using this technique faces several important considerations. As students view "Kubla Khan," have them watch for how the filmmaker handled each of these elements:

- how the chosen photographs accompany the lines of poetry
- how the chosen music accompanies the narration and images
- how the reader interprets the lines

(You may wish to have students use the Viewer's Guide on page 26 to record their observations.)

COMPARING TEXT AND PERFORMANCE

Encourage students to look for the similarities and differences between the poem"Kubla Khan" and the one they are about to view, especially noting the following aspects:

- how the experience of listening to poetry differs from reading it
- how images, music, and reading can affect the viewer's interpretation of a poem

LITERARY ANALYSIS IN MEDIA

Imagery In literature, imagery refers to the words or phrases that a writer uses to create vivid sensory experiences for the reader. Video conveys imagery directly to viewers in ways that printed words cannot. As students view the montage, encourage them to note the images chosen to illustrate the poem and to question whether the photographs support, complement, or detract from the words.

After Viewing

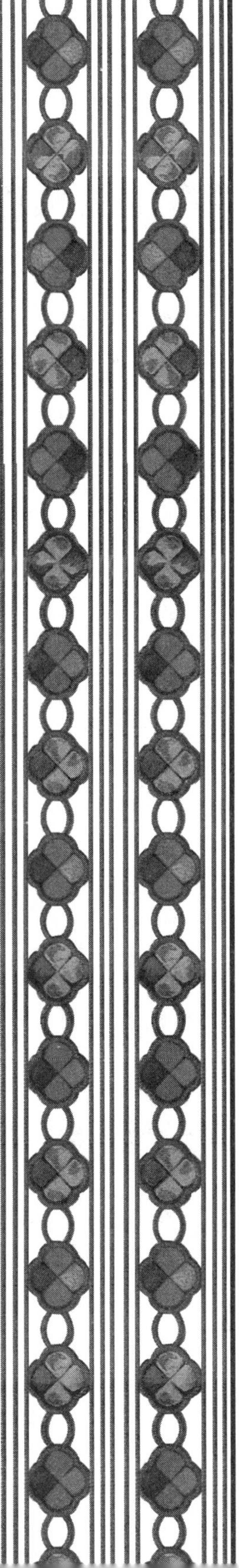

Use these prompts to initiate discussion:

WHAT DO YOU THINK?

1. What image or images in the video were the most memorable, and why? (Answers will vary.)

FOCUS FOR VIEWING

2. **The Art of Montage** What do you think of the images, reading style, and music chosen to convey the poem? Explain which aspects you think were particularly effective or ineffective. (Answers will vary.)

COMPARING TEXT AND PERFORMANCE

3. **Listening to Poetry** How did your experience of listening to "Kubla Khan" differ from reading it? Did hearing the poem change your understanding of it? (Students may say that listening to the poem helped them appreciate the words and the rhyme in the poem.)
4. **Interpretation** How did the images, music, and reading affect your interpretation of the poem? (Some students may say that the images and reading brought the words of the poem to life. The music added a tranquil feeling.) How could different choices in these three areas affect your understanding of the poem? (Answers will vary.)

LITERARY ANALYSIS IN MEDIA

5. **Imagery** Describe three of the photographs chosen to illustrate the poem. Did they support, complement, or detract from the lines? (Example: Students may say that the image of Kubla Khan helped them picture the leader of Xanadu or that the picture of the cavern did not do justice to the poem's description.)

LESSON ACTIVITIES

- **Writing Option: Journal Entry** Ask students to write a brief journal entry that depicts a vision of paradise, describing it as vividly as they can. They may illustrate the vision with drawings, photos, or cut-outs from a magazine.
- **Viewer's Guide: The Art of Montage** You may wish to have students use the copymaster on page 26 to note their observations of the images, music, and reading chosen for "Kubla Khan."

Name: ______________________________ Date: ______________

VIEWER'S GUIDE

THE ART OF MONTAGE

As you view "Kubla Khan," think about the images, music, and narration chosen to convey the poem. How effectively do you think these elements reflect the content of the poem? Use the chart below to record your observations. For each image, explain why it helps or hinders your understanding of the lines.

Images	Describe your impressions
A stately pleasure dome	
Five miles meandering with a mazy motion	
His flashing eyes, his floating hair!	
Music and Reading	
• Describe the music. What effect does it have on you?	
• Describe the narrator's reading style. What is effective or ineffective about it?	

The Lady of Shalott

A READING OF THE POEM WITH DRAWINGS

"Illustration is not so much a job as a way of life."

—CHARLES KEEPING, ILLUSTRATOR OF "THE LADY OF SHALOTT"

LESSON AT A GLANCE

Overview

Ink drawings and music are set to a reading of Alfred, Lord Tennyson's narrative poem "The Lady of Shalott."

Running Time: 11:00

Connecting to *The Language of Literature*

Show this reading of the poem with drawings after students read "The Lady of Shalott" in Unit 5, Part 1.

Objectives

- To compare Tennyson's poem with the television production
- To learn how to interpret art
- To understand how mood is created through art and voice

Lesson Activities

- Writing Option: Director's Notes (page 29)
- Viewer's Guide: Interpreting Art (page 30)

Before Viewing

Additional Resources: Alfred, Lord Tennyson

The Lady of Shalott
An artist, a historian, and a former prison inmate give their interpretations of Tennyson's "The Lady of Shalott." This video includes the performance of the poem that appears on the *Literature in Performance* videotape. *(Videocassette, 20 minutes, 1995; distributor: Films for the Humanities, (800) 257-5126)*

The Circle of the Hills
This documentary on Tennyson follows his life from childhood to his status as poet laureate, when his popularity rivaled that of a rock star. Excerpts and readings punctuate the historical images in the film. *(Videocassette, 61 minutes, 1992; distributor: Filmic Archives, (800) 366-1920)*

BUILDING BACKGROUND

In this presentation, an oral reading of Alfred, Lord Tennyson's classic poem "The Lady of Shalott" is illustrated with drawings. British actress Charlotte Cornwell reads the poem. The drawings, which were originally part of a children's book, were done by Charles Keeping, an illustrator, writer, and designer. Keeping had a deep admiration for "The Lady of Shalott" and other Victorian classics. His sepia-toned ink drawings are brought to life by camera techniques in this Thames Television production.

FOCUS FOR VIEWING

Interpreting Art Tell students that artists use many elements of design to communicate meaning. For example, in "The Lady of Shalott," Keeping used lines and shapes to render simple, romantic drawings in sepia-toned ink. These images convey a sad, sweet, and serene mood. Explain these artistic elements to students:

- A **line** is the basic foundation of design. Lines may vary in weight, width, and emphasis.
- A **shape** is created by lines that merge, touch, and intersect one another. Shapes take on many forms including rectangular, round, oval, and triangular.
- **Value** describes the light and dark elements in a pictorial design. Compositions with sharply contrasting values are usually more dramatic.

Have students note these elements of design as they view the television production. (You may wish to refer to the Viewer's Guide on page 30.)

COMPARING TEXT AND PERFORMANCE

Encourage students to think about the similarities and differences between reading Tennyson's "The Lady of Shalott" and watching and listening to this presentation. Have them especially note the following aspects:

- hearing the lines of the poem versus reading the lines silently
- seeing the drawings versus imagining the scenes

LITERARY ANALYSIS IN MEDIA

Mood In literature, mood refers to the feeling, or atmosphere, that a writer creates for the reader. Writers use imagery, figurative language, and rhythm to set a mood. Filmmakers have other tools for establishing a mood. Have students note the mood in the video and think about how it is established cinematically.

After Viewing

Use these prompts to initiate discussion:

WHAT DO YOU THINK?

1. What did you like about this presentation of Tennyson's poem? What didn't you like? (Some students may appreciate the drawings and find the illustrator's interpretation interesting. Others may have envisioned the Lady in a different way.)

FOCUS FOR VIEWING

2. **Interpreting Art** Describe three of Keeping's drawings that particularly interested you and explain why they interested you. (Students may describe the lady in the boat and note how peaceful and delicate she looks. They may mention the shape of the boat and the woman's soft curves and mystical facial expression.)

COMPARING TEXT AND PERFORMANCE

3. **Listening Versus Reading** How did listening to the poem influence your understanding of it? (Students may say that hearing the softness of the reader's voice and the rhythm of the lines prompted a sympathetic response.)
4. **Seeing Versus Imagining** Select one drawing that was unlike your own visualization of the scene in the poem and describe the differences. (Some students may think the illustrations were dreamlike, not realistic. Others may say that some elements of the poem were missing, like the loom or the inside of the Lady's tower.)

LITERARY ANALYSIS IN MEDIA

5. **Mood** Describe the mood in this presentation of "The Lady of Shalott." How was the mood established? Think about the style of the reading and the effect of the drawings. (Answers will vary, but some students may describe the narrator's rhythmic speech and the shadowy artistic style, which established a bittersweet mood.)

LESSON ACTIVITIES

- **Writing Option: Director's Notes** Ask students to imagine they are the film director for "The Lady of Shalott." Have students write a note to the artist explaining the ideas, the look, and the mood they want the artist to convey in the drawings.
- **Viewer's Guide: Interpreting Art** Students may use the copymaster on page 30 to interpret the drawings in "The Lady of Shalott."

Name: ______________________ Date: ____________

VIEWER'S GUIDE

INTERPRETING ART

Would you believe that dozens of artists have interpreted "The Lady of Shalott" in drawings and paintings? These artists were inspired to create exotic and beautiful images of the Lady. In this production, illustrator Charles Keeping used lines, shapes, and value to create two-tone drawings that evoke the content of the poem. View the presentation and study the following drawings. In the space next to each drawing, write your thoughts about the image.

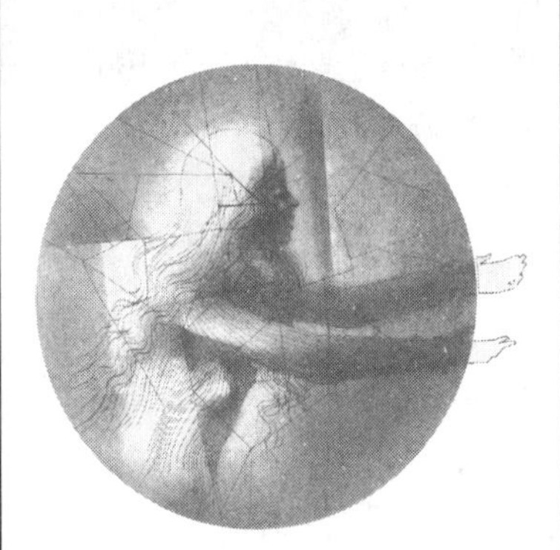	How does framing the Lady within a cracked mirror help convey the tragedy of this scene?
	What do the Lady's posture and facial expression convey?
	What mood is expressed in this illustration? Notice the white figure of the Lady. How are light and dark elements used by the artist?

The Rocking Horse Winner

A FILM ADAPTATION BY JOHN MILLS

"And so the house came to be haunted by the unspoken phrase: *There must be more money! There must be more money!*"

—FROM "THE ROCKING-HORSE WINNER" BY D.H. LAWRENCE

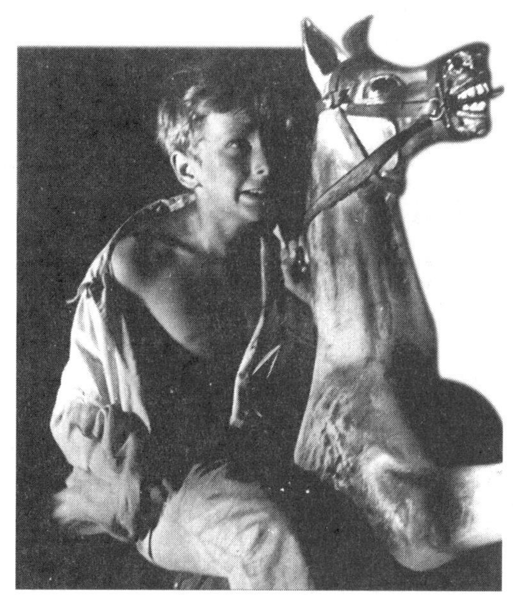

LESSON AT A GLANCE

Overview
This film excerpt features the final scenes of a 1949 adaptation of D.H. Lawrence's short story "The Rocking-Horse Winner."

Running Time: 15:30

Connecting to *The Language of Literature*
Show this film excerpt after students read "The Rocking-Horse Winner" in Unit 6, Part 1.

Objectives
- To compare the short story "The Rocking-Horse Winner" with the film adaptation
- To understand how suspense is developed in a film
- To analyze the effect of music and lighting in a film
- To examine the composition of scenes in a film

Lesson Activities
- Writing Option: Write a New Ending (page 34)
- Viewer's Guide: Music and Lighting in Film (page 35)
- Extension Activity: Understanding Composition (page 36)

Before Viewing

Movie poster advertising the 1949 film

BUILDING BACKGROUND

This excerpt shows the final scenes of the 1949 film adaptation of D.H. Lawrence's short story "The Rocking-Horse Winner." When originally released in theaters, *The Rocking Horse Winner* was described as "one of those flawlessly produced British movies." The film was written and directed by Anthony Pelissier of Great Britain. While keeping the original characters and most of the scenes from the short story, Pelissier altered some of the characterizations and expanded the plot, which is especially evident in the ending. The well-known British actor John Mills produced the film and also played the role of Bassett. Pelissier and Mills had previously teamed up to film other classics of British literature. Mills chose Lawrence's work to produce because he took joy in the knowledge that he was tackling a worthwhile subject.

Produced in black and white like other movies of the period, the film follows the style of a suspense thriller or horror film. One critic said that Pelissier "brought to visual fulfillment all of the haunting terror of a 10-year-old, sensitive boy so obsessed by his parents' need for funds that he drives himself to death."

TAPPING PRIOR KNOWLEDGE

Thinking About the Text Ask students to reread the ending of "The Rocking-Horse Winner." Tell them that filmmakers often change the ending of stories when they adapt a work of literature to film. Have students generate ideas for at least three different endings for the film of this story. Then have them rank the endings based on personal preference, using a chart like the one below to record their ideas.

Possible endings	Ranking

This film adaptation is excerpted from *The Rocking Horse Winner. (Videocassette, 90 minutes, 1949; distributor: Films for the Humanities, (800) 257-5126)*

FOCUS FOR VIEWING

Music and Lighting in Film Tell students that music and lighting in film serve many purposes. Music may be used to set the mood and atmosphere. Lighting may be used to provide depth and visual dimension in a scene. Have students recall recent movies they have seen, citing examples of the following uses of music and lighting:

- A rhythmic, dynamic piece of music may accompany a chase scene to reinforce screen action or heighten dramatic tension.
- Soft, sweet music can convey mood in a romantic scene.
- Focused, highly directed light can produce intense shadows as it strikes objects or characters in a suspense scene.
- Bright, or high, lighting is employed in dramatic scenes where dialogue and action are critical.

As students view *The Rocking Horse Winner,* have them note the effects of the music and lighting in specific scenes. (You may wish to have students use the Viewer's Guide on page 35 to note their observations.)

COMPARING TEXT AND PERFORMANCE

Ask students to look for similarities and differences between the ending of the short story and the film adaptation they will view, especially noting the following comparisons:

- how the ending was changed in the film and its effect
- how Paul's mother was portrayed

LITERARY ANALYSIS IN MEDIA

Suspense Suspense is the tension or excitement readers feel as they are drawn into a story and become increasingly eager to learn the outcome of the plot. Just as an author combines many elements to the create suspense in a story, a filmmaker uses a combination of elements to provide suspense in a film, including the following:

- plot
- dialogue
- camera angles
- lighting
- music

Encourage students to consider this question as they view the film: What techniques does the filmmaker use to heighten the suspense?

Additional Resources: The Theme of Greed

The Rocking Horse Winner
This 1977 film version of D.H. Lawrence's short story was filmed in England. It modernizes the setting of the 1949 film while retaining the power of the ideas and symbols of the story. This film is also available in Spanish. *(Videocassette, 30 minutes, 1977; distributor: Phoenix/Coronet, (800) 221-1274)*

Greed
An Erich von Stroheim silent film, based on the novel *McTeague* by Frank Norris, takes a look at the personal and societal costs of the pursuit of money. *(Videocassette, 133 minutes, 1924; distributor: Critics' Choice Video, (800) 367-7765)*

After Viewing

Use these prompts to initiate discussion after viewing:

WHAT DO YOU THINK?

1. What was your first reaction to the ending of the film? (Answers will vary.)

FOCUS FOR VIEWING

2. **Music and Lighting in Film** Give specific examples of the music and lighting in the film. What was their effect? (The pace of the music quickened as the mother ascended the stairs to Paul's room, creating a sense of suspense and drama; the darkness and the shadows cast in Paul's room reinforced the eerie mood.)

COMPARING TEXT AND PERFORMANCE

3. **The Ending** How did the ending of the film differ from the ending of the story, and what effect did the new ending have? (The film extended the story beyond Paul's death and showed Paul's mother ordering Bassett to burn the money. Bassett refused and decided to give it to charity. The new ending changed the moral of the story and portrayed Paul's mother as repentant.)
4. **The Mother** How did the portrayal of the mother in the film differ from the portrayal of her in the story? (The mother was portrayed more sympathetically in the film. She appeared to deeply love Paul, she felt tremendous regret and guilt over her role in his death, and she no longer valued money more than people.)

LITERARY ANALYSIS IN MEDIA

5. **Suspense** Describe the techniques the filmmaker used to heighten suspense. (The filmmaker included dramatic music, used subdued lighting, dark shadows, and close-ups on characters' faces.)

LESSON ACTIVITIES

- **Writing Option: Write a New Ending** Have students choose an idea they generated for an ending to *The Rocking Horse Winner* before viewing the film. Have them use the idea to write their own ending to the film.
- **Viewer's Guide: Music and Lighting in Film** Use the copymaster on page 35 to help students analyze the effects of the music and lighting in the film.
- **Extension Activity: Understanding Composition** Use the copymaster on page 36 to help students examine the composition of scenes in the film.

Name: ______________________________ Date: ______________

VIEWER'S GUIDE

MUSIC AND LIGHTING IN FILM

Filmmakers often use music and lighting to create a mood, add suspense, emphasize a theme, or achieve other effects in a film. View *The Rocking Horse Winner* and pay attention to the music and lighting. Use the chart below to record your observations of the music and lighting used in two of the scenes.

Scene	Music	Lighting
Mother ascending stairs and moving down hall to Paul's room	Describe the music.	Describe the lighting.
	What was its effect?	What was its effect?
Deathbed scene between Paul and his mother	Describe the music.	Describe the lighting.
	What was its effect?	What was its effect?

Name: ______________________________ Date: ____________

EXTENSION ACTIVITY

UNDERSTANDING COMPOSITION

In filmmaking, the term composition refers to the use of light and camera angles and the arrangement of objects and characters within a film frame to achieve particular effects. When composing a frame, the filmmaker considers the effect of the following elements:

- the **position** of objects and characters in a film frame
- the **movement** of objects and characters in a film frame
- the **lighting**, such as low-key lighting that emphasizes shadows
- the **camera angles**, such as low camera angle that emphasizes an object

Below are two film frames from *The Rocking Horse Winner.* Describe what you observe about the composition of each and the effects.

Mother discovering Paul

Describe the composition of this scene. What is the effect of the positions of Paul, his mother, and the shadow of the horse?

Uncle deciding to place bet

What is the effect of the phone in the foreground and the uncle in the background? How does the camera angle contribute to the effect?

Film Terms Glossary

CINEMATOGRAPHY The art or technique of motion-picture photography.

CLOSE-UP A SHOT that shows a magnified view of a person or object. A close-up of a character usually shows only his or her head.

COMPOSITION The use of lighting, camera angles, and arrangements of objects and characters within a film frame to achieve particular effects.

CUT An abrupt transition from one SHOT to another.

DEEP-FOCUS SHOT A SHOT filmed in such a way that all the objects and people in the scene are in focus, no matter how close to or far away from the camera they are.

DISSOLVE A transitional technique in which one scene or image FADES out as another fades in, so that the first seems to disappear as the second appears.

DOCUMENTARY A nonfiction film focusing on a historical, scientific, social, or environmental subject. The purpose of a documentary may be to educate, to persuade, or to provide insight into the world in which we live.

DOLLY SHOT or **TRACKING SHOT** A shot that moves toward or away from a person or object. Also a shot that moves alongside a moving figure or object. These effects are achieved by pushing or pulling the camera on a dolly (DOLLY SHOT) or on a vehicle that runs on tracks (TRACKING SHOT). See also ZOOM SHOT.

EDITING The arrangement of a number of SHOTS in sequence to form a complete film.

ESTABLISHING SHOT A SHOT that serves to introduce viewers to the location of a scene, usually by presenting a wide view of an area. See also LONG SHOT or EXTREME LONG SHOT.

EXTREME LONG SHOT A SHOT in which a large area, such as a vast desert or a city skyline, is filmed from a great distance to provide a panoramic view of it. See also ESTABLISHING SHOT.

FADE A technique in which a scene or image seems to disappear gradually into black (fade out) or to appear gradually out of black (fade in).

FREEZE-FRAME An effect that stops (freezes) the motion in a scene, so that the image on screen looks like a still photograph.

HAND-HELD SHOT A SHOT in which the camera is held and moved by its operator instead of being attached to a mechanical support. Often resulting in unsteady images and jerky camera movements, this technique is sometimes used to film a POINT-OF-VIEW SHOT or to create a spontaneous, free style in a film.

HIGH-ANGLE SHOT A SHOT that shows a scene from above.

HIGH-KEY LIGHTING A style of lighting in which all the objects and people in a scene are brightly and evenly lit, with few conspicuous shadows.

LONG SHOT A SHOT that provides a wide view of a scene, showing many objects and/or people at once. See also ESTABLISHING SHOT and EXTREME LONG SHOT.

LOW-ANGLE SHOT A SHOT filmed from below eye level.

LOW-KEY LIGHTING A style of lighting characterized by strong contrasts between light and dark, pronounced shadows, and often atmospheric pools of light.

MEDIUM SHOT A SHOT that shows a view wider than a CLOSE–UP but less wide than a LONG SHOT. A medium shot of one or more characters usually shows them from the knees or waist up.

MONTAGE A succession of SHOTS, often short and lacking dialogue, that is intended to create a particular effect or convey a particular meaning. In the film *Forrest Gump*, for example, the montage showing Forrest Gump running across America conveys the passage of time and Gump's growing popularity.

PAN A SHOT that scans across a location (left to right or vice versa). A pan is achieved by rotating a camera horizontally on a stationary base.

POINT–OF–VIEW SHOT A SHOT that shows what a character sees.

REACTION SHOT A SHOT that shows a character reacting to another character's dialogue or movement.

SHOOTING SCRIPT A script that contains not only dialogue and descriptions of action, but also detailed technical instructions for all of a film's SHOTS.

SHOT The continuous recording of a scene or image, from the time the camera starts to the time it stops.

STORYBOARD A device sometimes used to plan the shooting of a film and to help the filmmaker envision what the finished product will look like. It consists of a sequence of sketches showing what will appear in the film's SHOTS, often with explanatory notes and dialogue written beside or underneath them.

SUPERIMPOSITION An effect in which two or more SHOTS appear on the screen at the same time, creating the appearance of "layers" of images.

THREE SHOT A SHOT that shows three characters.

TILT A SHOT that scans a location with an upward or downward movement. A tilt is achieved by moving the camera vertically on a stationary base.

TWO SHOT A SHOT that shows two characters.

VOICEOVER Narration, commentary, or dialogue spoken by a character or person who does not appear in the scene it accompanies.

WIPE A transitional technique in which a line moving across the screen appears to "wipe away" one scene or image, replacing it with another.

ZOOM SHOT A SHOT in which an adjustable camera lens is used to provide an increasingly close view of the subject being filmed (zoom in) or an increasingly distant view of the subject (zoom out). In a zoom shot, unlike a DOLLY SHOT, the camera itself is not moved.

Resources for Teaching with Film

GENERAL REFERENCE

Amelio, Ralph J. *Film in the Classroom: Why Use It, How To Use It.* Dayton: Pflaum/ Standard, 1971. (773) 792-3824

Considine, David M. and Gail E. Haley. *Visual Messages: Integrating Imagery into Instruction.* 2nd ed. Englewood: Teacher Ideas Press, 1999. ISBN: 1563085755

Costanzo, William V. *Reading the Movies: Twelve Great Films on Video and How To Teach Them.* Urbana: National Council of Teachers of English, 1992. ISBN: 0814139108

Giannetti, Louis D. *Understanding Movies.* 8th ed. Upper Saddle River: Prentice Hall, 1999. ISBN: 0136465633

Heinich, Robert, Michael Molenda, and James D. Russell. *Instructional Media and Technologies for Learning.* 6th ed. Upper Saddle River: Prentice Hall, 1999. ISBN: 0138591598

Mast, Gerald and Bruce F. Kawin. *A Short History of the Movies.* 6th ed. Boston: Allyn and Bacon, 1996. ISBN: 0023770759

Resch, Kenneth E. and Vicki D. Schicker. *Using Film in the High School Curriculum: A Practical Guide for Teachers and Librarians.* Jefferson: McFarland & Co., 1992. ISBN: 0899507506

FILM AND VIDEO INDEXES

A-V Online. National Information Center for Educational Media. Available through SilverPlatter Information, Inc. on CD-ROM, Internet. (800) 343-0064

Film & Video Finder. 3 vol., 5th ed. Published for the National Information Center for Educational Media. Medford: Plexus, 1997. ISBN: 0937548294

Craddock, James M., ed., and Martin Connors. *VideoHound's Golden Movie Retriever.* Detroit: Visible Ink Press, 1998. ISBN: 1578590248

Craddock, James M., ed. *The Video Source Book.* 21st ed. Detroit: Gale Research, 1998. ISBN: 0787638579

FILM AND VIDEO SOURCES

AGC Educational Media
1560 Sherman Avenue
Suite 100
Evanston, IL 60201
(800) 323-9084

American Poetry Archives
San Francisco State University
1600 Holloway Avenue
San Francisco, CA 94132
(415) 338-1056

The Annenberg/CPB
Multimedia Collection
P.O. Box 2345
S. Burlington, VT 05407-2345
(800) 532-7637

Best Video
1697 Whitney Avenue
Hamden, CT 06517
(800) 873-2850

Critics' Choice Video
P.O. Box 749
Itasca, IL 60143-0479
(800) 367-7765

Facets Multimedia
1517 West Fullerton Avenue
Chicago, IL 60614
(800) 331-6197

Filmic Archives
The Cinema Center
Botsford, CT 06404-0386
(800) 366-1920

Films for the Humanities &
Sciences
P.O. Box 2053
Princeton, NJ 08543-2053
(800) 257-5126

LTV Literary Television
934 Brannan Street, 2nd floor
San Francisco, CA 94103
(415) 267-4887

the monterey movie company
566 St. Charles Drive
Thousand Oaks, CA 91360
(800) 424-2593

Movies Unlimited
3015 Darnell Road
Philadelphia, PA 19154-3295
(800) 466-8437

Phoenix Learning Group
2349 Chaffee Drive
St. Louis, MO 63146
(800) 221-1274

Pyramid Media
P.O. Box 1048
Santa Monica, CA 90406-1048
(800) 421-2304

SVE (Society for Visual Education) & Churchill Media
6677 North Northwest Highway
Chicago, IL 60631-1304
(800) 829-1900

PROFESSIONAL ORGANIZATIONS AND PUBLICATIONS

Assembly of Media Arts
National Council of Teachers of English
11 West Kenyon Road
Urbana, IL 61801
(800) 369-6283
Newsletter: *Media Matters*

Association for Media Literacy
1 Aberfoyle Crescent #2204
Toronto, Ontario M8X2X8
Canada
(416) 696-7144
Newsletter: *Mediacy*

Center for Media Literacy
4727 Wilshire Boulevard, #403
Los Angeles, CA 90010
(800) 226-9494

National Communication Association
5105 Backlick Road, Building E
Annandale, VA 22003
(703) 750-0533
Publication: K-12 *Media Literacy Standards and Competency Statements*

National Telemedia Council
120 East Wilson Street
Madison, WI 53703
(608) 257-7712
Newsletter: *Telemedium*

FILM AND VIDEO PRODUCTION

Making Grimm Movies
Davenport Films
11324 Pearlstone Lane
Delaplane, VA 20144-1722
(540) 592-3701

Based on an award-winning series of movie folktales, the documentary *Making Grimm Movies* helps teachers and students learn the basics of moviemaking.

Fiction to Film—
A Three-Part Series
This series pairs a film adaptation of a Steinbeck short story with a short film about the making of the adaptation.

The Raid
Lighting the Action: The Making of John Steinbeck's "The Raid"

The Chrysanthemums
Behind the Camera: The Making of John Steinbeck's "The Chrysanthemums"

Molly Morgan
Editing the Scene: The Making of John Steinbeck's "Molly Morgan"

Available from:
Pyramid Media
P.O. Box 1048
Santa Monica, CA 90406-1048
(800) 421-2304

Name: ______________________ Date: __________

VIEWING ACTIVITY 1

COMPARING AND CONTRASTING TEXT AND PERFORMANCE

What did you view? ______________________

1. What are the major similarities between the text and the performance? What are the major differences?

2. Were any important parts of the text not conveyed in the performance? If so, how did their omission affect the way in which the performance represented the text?

3. What did the performance contain that is not in the text? Do you think that the additional elements were wisely chosen? Why or why not?

4. Which did you find more enjoyable and meaningful—the text or the performance? Why?

5. If you were creating a performance based on the text, what features would your performance have in addition to what is in the text? What elements of the text might you change or omit? Why?

Name: ______________________________ Date: ______________

VIEWING ACTIVITY 2

EVALUATING A FILM OR PERFORMANCE

What did you view? ______________________________

1. Briefly describe the film or performance.

____

____

____

____

2. Describe the opening of the film or performance. Explain why it did or did not "pull you in."

____

____

____

____

3. If more than one character or performer appeared, which one did you find most appealing? Why?

____

____

____

____

4. What did you learn from the film or performance?

____

____

____

____

5. On a five-star scale (with five the highest), how do you rate the film or performance? Why?

____

____

____

____

Name: ______________________ Date: __________

VIEWING ACTIVITY 3

ANALYZING A FILM

What did you view? ______________________

1. Briefly describe the film.

2. How were music and sound effects used?

3. What effects were created by the lighting?

4. Describe any establishing (long) shots. Why do you think the filmmaker included them?

5. Describe any close-up or zoom shots. Why do you think the filmmaker included them?

6. Was the dialogue believable? Why or why not? Give an example.

7. On the back of this paper, describe your other impressions of the film.

Answer Key

THE BATTLE WITH GRENDEL

Viewer's Guide (page 7)
Words Answers may include that the storyteller said Beowulf "could outwrestle a bear;" the storyteller described Grendel as "Grendel, a monster, a foul fiend." "He [Beowulf] began to twist the monster's arm." "You could hear the bones crack and break."

Delivery Tone of voice used for characters: Answers may include Beowulf—confident, bold, forceful; Grendel—greedy, fiendish, evil; the king—grateful, loving, amazed. Pace and volume: As the battle between Beowulf and Grendel proceeded, the storyteller increased the pace of his speech and the volume of his voice until it climaxed with a scream. After the battle, the storyteller resumed a slower delivery and a calmer tone.

Body Language Gestures: The storyteller held up his hands as he said that Beowulf would use his hands to kill Grendel. Postures: The storyteller stood proudly erect as he listed Beowulf's acts of bravery. Facial expressions: The storyteller's face grimaced as he talked about Grendel's pain when his arm was ripped off.

Extension Activity (page 8)
Answers to the Planning Guide activity will vary depending on the students' choice of story and decisions on how to perform the story. Their performances should reflect what they learned from watching the storyteller dramatize *The Battle with Grendel.*

THE PARDONER'S TALE

Viewer's Guide (page 13)
Script Answers may include that the filmmaker decided to keep the language in the film identical to the wording in Chaucer's story to make the film an authentic adaptation of the story.

Cast Answers may include that the different sizes and shapes of the three rioters (one was large and heavy set with a beard, one was small with a mustache, and the other was tall and skinny) helped capture the comic character of Chaucer's poem. Casting Gielgud, a very dignified actor, as the narrator strengthened both the moral and comic tones of the tale.

Costumes Answers will vary but may include that the use of modern costumes gave the story a more timeless feel.

Settings Answers may include that the settings of the old stone inn, the quaint English village with old buildings, and the countryside helped to give the film an authentic medieval quality.

Extension Activity (page 14)
The scenes that the student teams develop will differ depending on their interests and choices. Their adaptations should reflect what they have learned from the film adaptation of *The Pardoner's Tale.*

MACBETH

Viewer's Guide (page 19)
Macbeth and Banquo riding up to the witches Shot: The shot is an establishing shot. Effects: To show the setting of the witches scene, including the fog, the pools of water, and the strange rock formations, and to add mystery and suspense to the scene.

Macbeth and Banquo confronting the witches Shots: Various shots are used in this scene—an establishing shot, medium shots, and a close-up. Effects: Answers will vary but may include that these shots let you see the setting in which the scene takes place, the action between Macbeth and Banquo and the witches, and close-ups of the clay figure of Macbeth.

Macbeth speaking with men on horseback Shots: This scene includes medium shots and close-up shots. Effects: The medium shots let you see the action between the men, while the close-up shots allow you to see their facial expressions, revealing their emotions and thoughts.

Macbeth's aside Shot: This scene consists of an extreme close-up shot. Effects: This shot lets you see the intensity of Macbeth's thoughts and emotions during the voiceover narration.

Ending view of the witches Shot: This is a low-angle establishing shot. Effects: Filming the witches from below adds to the mystery, suspense, and bizarreness of the scene. There is a sense that the witches will reign over Macbeth's future.

Extension Activity 1 (page 20)
Welles's *Macbeth*

Setting A foggy moor with pools of water and strange rock formations.

Witches There was never a clear shot of the faces of the witches. They were portrayed as three misshapen creatures; whether they were human was unclear.

Macbeth Welles portrayed Macbeth as a strong, confident, arrogant character who showed little doubt about the witches' prophecies.

Language Welles took great liberty with the language in this adaptation of *Macbeth*. Lines were moved around and scenes were re-arranged.

RSC's *Macbeth*

Setting The stage of a theater.

Witches The close-ups of the witches in this production showed them to be actual women of different ages and sizes.

Macbeth McKellen portrayed Macbeth as fearful, troubled, and plagued with self-doubt.

Language The language of this performance matched that of the play.

Extension Activity 2 (page 21)
Answers will vary.

Extension Activity 3 (page 22)
Answers will vary depending on the students' reactions to the actors' performances and on their interpretation of the play's meaning.

KUBLA KHAN

Viewer's Guide (page 26)
Image of a stately pleasure dome Impressions: Answers will vary but may include that this image of an Asian palace matched the words in the poem and helps the understanding of the poem.

Image of a meandering river Impressions: Answers may include that the picture of a flowing stream worked as a metaphor for the lines in the poem but did not entirely fit the language. Meandering means "to wander aimlessly," while the stream in the picture was rushing quickly in its bed.

Image of a statue of Kubla Khan Impressions: Answers may include that although the picture of the statue depicted Kubla Khan, it did not match or express the phrase "his flashing eyes, his floating hair."

Music Answers may include that the music was melancholy and flowing like a river, and that it fit the setting of the poem. Students may say it brought them into the mood of the poem.

Reading Answers will vary but may include that the narrator's reading style worked well with the poem. The words were nicely pronounced, read at a good pace, and her tone matched the character of the poem. However, students may also note that the reading was serene in nature, and therefore did not express some of the wilder or more violent aspects of the poem.

THE LADY OF SHALOTT

Viewer's Guide (page 30)
Image of the Lady, trapped Answers may include that the framing emphasized that the Lady was trapped. She was caught within the frame of the

cracked mirror just as she was caught within the curse.

Image of the Lady, seated Answers may include that the Lady's slumped shoulders, bowed head, and somber expression showed that she was sad, dejected, and melancholy.

Image of the castle and Lady The mood of the illustration was ominous, mysterious, and scary. The darkness of the castle and the sky contrasted with the light figure of the Lady. This contrast gave the impression that the castle was foreboding and the spirit of the Lady was sweet and innocent.

THE ROCKING HORSE WINNER

Viewer's Guide (page 35)

Mother ascending stairs and moving down hall to Paul's room Music: The music began fast paced, reached a climax, then stopped before gradually building to another climax. Effect: The music was suspenseful and foreboding, sounding like a frantic race. Lighting: As the mother ascended the stairs, she cast a strong shadow on the wall. When the mother reached the hall, she was well lit, but the hall in front of her was dark. She walked through the dark hall and reached a door, where she was lit, but darkness surrounded her. Effect: Answers may include that the shadows set a scary mood. The darkness in the hall suggested that she was approaching something horrible. The darkness surrounding the mother implied that she was surrounded by something terrible.

Deathbed scene between Paul and his mother Music: The music was soothing, quiet, sad, and mournful. Effect: Answers may include that the music lead the viewer to feel sad and sorry for Paul. The music also suggested the mother's regret. Lighting: The lighting cast heavy shadows. Bedridden Paul was more brightly lit than the rest of the room. Effect: Answers may include that the lighting gave the scene a somber, serious mood. The lightness around Paul suggested an otherworldly feel.

Extension Activity (page 36)

Mother discovering Paul Paul was in the foreground on the floor as the shadow of the rocking horse loomed in the background and his mother was positioned over and behind him. The large, eerie shadow of the rocking horse pointed at the mother as she hurried toward Paul in the foreground. The shadow hovered like an evil spirit over Paul. These positions showed that the spirit had won. The composition, the low angle shot, and the heavy shadows added tension and suspense to the scene.

Uncle deciding to place bet The phone loomed large in the lower right foreground. It beckoned to the conflicted uncle who turned his head toward it though his back was turned away from it. The camera angle—up toward the uncle from the phone—created the sense that the phone represented temptation. The composition of this shot illustrated the tension the Uncle was feeling about whether to place another bet. The phone was a powerful symbol in the scene and showed the uncle's struggle with the moral dilemma that the phone call represented.

Acknowledgments

VIDEO

The Battle with Grendel: Produced by Rymel Multimedia. Copyright © 1997 McDougal Littell Inc. All rights reserved.

The Pardoner's Tale: Segment provided courtesy of Films for the Humanities and Sciences. All rights reserved.

Macbeth (Welles): Licensed by the Estate of Orson Welles. All rights reserved. Represented by Thomas A. White, Beverly Hills, California. Footage from *Macbeth* provided courtesy of Republic Entertainment, Inc., and Digital Matters. Music by Jacques Ibert, copyright © MCA Music Publishing, a division of Universal Studios, Inc. (100%).

Macbeth (Royal Shakespeare Company): Segment provided courtesy of Films for the Humanities and Sciences. All rights reserved.

Kubla Khan: Produced by Rymel Multimedia. Copyright © 1997 McDougal Littell Inc. All rights reserved. Images courtesy of National Palace Museum, Taiwan/E.T. Archive, London/SuperStock; Nicole Nelson; © Michael Mathers/Peter Arnold, Inc.; W. Woodworth/SuperStock; C. Orrico/SuperStock; © Kevin Schafer/Peter Arnold, Inc.; M. Thonig/SuperStock; M. Sands/SuperStock; V. Sigl/SuperStock; © James H. Karales/Peter Arnold, Inc.; SuperStock; Mia & Klaus Matthes/SuperStock; Rhonda Krafchin; Van Hoorick/SuperStock; L. A. Huff/SuperStock; R. Llewellyn/SuperStock; W. D. Murphy/SuperStock; M. Keller/SuperStock.

The Lady of Shalott: Segment provided courtesy of Films for the Humanities and Sciences. All rights reserved.

The Rocking Horse Winner: Segment provided courtesy of Films for the Humanities and Sciences. All rights reserved.

ART

3, 4 Syd Lieberman; **9** Corbis-Bettmann; **10, 15** *right* Pearson Television Stills Library; **15** *left* Licensed by the estate of Orson Welles. All rights reserved. Represented by Thomas A. White, Beverly Hills, California. Provided courtesy of Republic Entertainment, Inc., and Digital Matters; **16** Films for the Humanities and Sciences; **23** Copyright © Wan-go Weng; **26** *top* Nicole Nelson; *center* SuperStock; *bottom* Nicole Nelson; **27, 30** *top*, *center*, *bottom* Illustrations by Charles Keeping taken from *The Lady of Shalott*, by permission of Oxford University Press; **31** Kobal Collection; **36** *top*, *bottom* Films for the Humanities and Sciences.